of this work have add
factual material herein
following: unique
coordination, expres:
classification of the in:
publication will be vigo.......... ....

C000063840

Copyright © 2001
Gale Group, Inc.
27500 Drake Road
Farmington Hills, MI 48331-3535

ISBN 0-7876-4085-9
ISSN 1094-9232

Printed in the United States of America.
10 9 8 7 6 5 4 3 2 1

Ghosts

Henrik Ibsen 1882

Introduction

Henrik Ibsen's *Ghosts* surprises modern audiences with some of the issues that it discusses, including out-of-wedlock children, venereal disease, incest, infidelity, and euthanasia. It is the story of a woman, Mrs. Alving, who is preparing for the opening of an orphanage in memory of her husband, Captain Alving, on the tenth anniversary of his death. The captain was an important and respected man in his community, and Mrs. Alving plans to raise this one great memorial to him so that she will not have to ever again speak of him. She wants to avoid the awful truth: that he was a cheating, immoral philanderer whose public reputation was a sham. Their son Oswald has come home from Paris with the news that he is dying of syphilis, which he contracted in the womb, and planning to marry the family's maid. He hopes that she can nurse him as his illness progresses, and Mrs. Alving has to tell him that the maid is actually Captain Alving's illegitimate daughter.

The "ghosts" in this play are the taboo topics that cannot be openly discussed. This drama is one of Ibsen's most powerful works, but also one of his most controversial. Its initial publication sold only a few copies, with most of those printed returned to the publisher and no new edition printed until thirteen years later. It was not performed in Ibsen's native Norway for almost a decade after its world debut in Chicago. In 1898, at a dinner in Ibsen's honor at the Royal Palace in Stockholm, King Oscar II expressed the opinion that *Ghosts* was not a good play, and that Ibsen should not have written it. After a moment of silence, the playwright replied, "Your majesty, I had to write *Ghosts*."

Henrik Ibsen was born in 1828 to a wealthy family in Skien, on the east coast of Norway. His father's ancestors had been seafarers; his mother came from a family of the most prominent merchants in the town. During the early years of his life, Ibsen grew up in luxury. His father owned one of the most prosperous stores in Skein, and the family had servants and a stable of horses and a house in the country. That changed early in the author's life, in 1835, when a drop in timber prices forced his father into bankruptcy. The store was lost, the house was sold at auction, and the family had to move to a rented house outside of town. Many critics point to the sudden reversal in his family's fortune as a key to Ibsen's later cynicism about the social order.

After the family's fall from social prestige, life became difficult in the Ibsen household. His father became a hot-tempered bully, constantly shouting and arguing. His mother, whom Ibsen adored, became silent and moody. Henrik became withdrawn, interested in reading and in producing puppet shows. He did not get along with many of the neighboring children, but when he did it was more often with the girls than with the boys.

Ibsen dropped out of school at age fifteen and worked for several years as a pharmacist's assistant. He went to Christiana (which has since become known as Oslo) in 1850 and attempted to enroll in

Christiana University, only to be rejected after failing the entrance exams in mathematics and Greek. He became an assistant stage manager at the National Theater in Bergen: one of his duties was to write patriotic plays that celebrated the national character of Norway. This was the beginning of his playwriting career.

Critics often divide Ibsen's plays into three groups or stages. The first stage of his writing, from the 1850s through the end of the 1860s, is marked by dry, traditional, nationalistic plays. These plays were often based in Norwegian legends, such as tales of the Vikings. *Ghosts* belongs to the second period, which is considered to be the most artistically productive. Starting from 1863, and for twenty-seven years after, he lived abroad in Italy and Germany, returning to Norway only once. The plays in this second period are realistic, driven by dialog and not theatrical conventions, while challenging social morality. Also included in this stage are the well-known plays *A Doll's House*(1879) and *An Enemy of the People*(1882). This phase of realism hit its high point with *Hedda Gabler* in 1890. The plays of his last period, during the 1890s, depart from the theme of the individual against society and deal with the individual alone. The most successful of these plays is *The Master Builder* from 1892, which many critics consider Ibsen's most autobiographical work. In 1901, Ibsen's writing career came to an end when he suffered the first of a series of paralyzing strokes. He died in Norway, on May 23, 1906, from complications from the strokes.

Plot Summary

Act I

Ghosts takes place in the library of the country house of Helena Alving, a wealthy widow. It opens with Mrs. Alving's maid, Regina Engstrand, being visited by Jacob Engstrand, who often reminds her that he is her father, although she seems to doubt it —he tells her that the church register can prove it. Engstrand has been working nearby as a carpenter, helping to build an orphanage, and when he returns to town, he wants Regina to go with him because he plans on using the money he has earned to open a boarding house for sailors and a tavern; and he wants a woman around: "But there must be a petticoat in the house... . For I want to have it a little lively in the evenings, with singing and dancing, and so forth." When Engstrand leaves, Pastor Manders enters. Engstrand has confided with the pastor about the drunken life he has led, and the pastor supports his new plan and thinks that Regina should be supportive of her father.

Mrs. Alving enters and discusses the plans of the orphanage with the pastor, who is her financial advisor. She is building the orphanage as a memorial to her late husband, who was an honored member of the community. The pastor suggests that the orphanage not be insured, because insuring it might make people doubt her trust in God.

Mrs. Alving's son Oswald, a painter, enters. He shocks the pastor with talk about couples living together and having children in Paris, where he has recently lived. When he steps out, Pastor Manning tells Mrs. Alving that she should be a better mother. He reminds her that she left Chamberlain Alving early in their marriage, but that after the pastor convinced her to return to her husband, Alving turned out to be a fine husband. She tells him that Alving was never faithful, that he had an affair with the maid, who was Regina's mother. At the end of the scene, she hears Oswald in the next room, making sexual advances toward Regina.

Act II

Later the same day, after dinner, Mrs. Alving and Pastor Manders talk about ending the flirtation between Oswald and Regina, who are brother and sister. She does not want to send Regina to live with Engstrand, who married a pregnant girl and raised her child for money. Engstrand enters and asks the pastor to lead a prayer meeting at the new orphanage. When Manders asks Engstrand about Regina, he explains that he did not personally profit, that the money given to Regina's mother was all spent on the child's education. He asks for the pastor's help with his planned home for sailors: "[I]t too might be a sort of orphanage, in a manner of speaking. There are many temptations for seafaring folk ashore. But in this Home of mine, a man might feel as under a father's eye, in a manner of speaking."

When they leave, Mrs. Alving talks to Oswald. He has been diagnosed with a disease—the play does not use the word syphilis, but the symptoms indicate it. A doctor has told him that the disease was probably with him since birth, although he does not believe that because he was raised to think that his father was morally correct. On his last visit, he says, he casually mentioned taking Regina to Paris for a trip, and on returning he has found out that she has planned her whole life around it. Mrs. Alving invites Regina to sit down with them and drink champagne with them just as Pastor Manders returns from the prayer at the orphanage. He is about to tell Oswald and Regina that they are related, but they look out the window and see that the orphanage is on fire.

Act III

Engstrand says that he saw Pastor Manders start the fire, that he snuffed out a candle and threw it among wood shavings, although the pastor does not remember even having held a candle. Mrs. Alving says that she has no intention of rebuilding the orphanage, that the pastor can do what he wants with the leftover money, and Engstrand suggests he use it to support the sailors' home. Mrs. Alving tells Oswald and Regina that Chamberlain Alving was Regina's father, and Regina is not surprised; instead, she turns out to be selfish, wanting to leave as soon as she knows that she cannot marry Oswald, unwilling to spend her days caring for a sick man. Mrs. Alving tells her that she is always welcome to return if she ever needs a home, and Regina responds that there is one place she knows she will always have a right to: the sailors' home.

> MRS ALVING: Regina—now I see it—you're going to your ruin.
> REGINA: Oh, stuff! Good-bye.

After Regina has gone, Mrs. Alving muses over the idea that she might not have been the victim of Chamberlain Alving's terrible behavior, but rather the cause of it, making him live in a small provincial town when he might have been more suited for a large city. She promises to take care of Oswald in his illness. Oswald shows her some pills that he was going to tell Regina to poison him with if the next attack of his illness destroyed his brain. As the sun comes up, he sits in a chair, facing away from the window, and says, "Mother, give me the sun." After that, he does not move and only repeats, "The sun. The sun." Mrs. Alving takes the box of pills from his pocket, and before she gives them to Oswald, the curtain falls.

Mrs. Helena Alving

Mrs. Alving is the widow of Captain Alving, a well-respected man in the community who has been dead for ten years. She is preparing to open an orphanage named after him to serve the nearby town. When Pastor Manders accuses her of failing to provide Oswald with enough moral guidance, he reminds Mrs. Alving that she has left her husband during her first year of marriage, but that he turned out all right after she returned to him. This prompts Mrs. Alving to tell the truth that she had kept hidden. Captain Alving was an awful man who was unfaithful throughout their marriage. The orphanage is to be built with all of the money Captain Alving had when he married her, and she will live on the money that she made from managing their investments after their marriage; in this way, she hopes to free herself of anything to do with him.

In the course of this play, Mrs. Alving loses her connection with conventional morality. She feels that social convention is false, and that she can put pretense behind her when she distances herself from Captain Alving's memory after naming the orphanage after him. In the last act, though, her view on life is turned around. Instead of seeing herself as a long-silent victim of Captain Alving's hedonistic ways, she sees that he was a victim of her.

Oswald Alving

Oswald is Mrs. Alving's son, who came home the day before the play begins. He has been living in Paris, where his work as an painter has been successful enough to earn coverage in the local Norwegian papers.

While Oswald was growing up, Mrs. Alving attempted to protect him from his father's bad influence by sending him away to school at an early age. The one memory of his father that Oswald talks about in the play is when he was a very young boy, and Captain Alving took him up on his knee and gave him his pipe to smoke. Seeing him smoking his father's pipe, Pastor Manders is shocked by how much Oswald looks like Captain Alving. Oswald has, in fact, grown up to be quite a lot like his father, in spite of his mother's attempts to prevent such a fate. He smokes, and he drinks, and he has relations with women outside of marriage. Soon after Mrs. Alving tells the pastor about her husband's affair with their maid, she finds Oswald carrying on with the present maid, just as his father did.

Jacob Engstrand

In some ways, Engstrand is the mirror image of the late Captain Alving, who is frequently talked about in this play but who died ten years before the play's time. Both men are drinkers and opportunists, willing to lie to secure their good names in society.

Mrs. Alving has hired Jacob to work on the orphanage, and he plans to use the money that he has earned to open a business in town. The purpose of the place changes—early in the first act, he refers to it as a "tavern" for sailors, though by the last act, when he is asking for funding from the pastor, he talks about the place as if it were a rest home for retired sailors, "sort of an Orphanage," which he presents as a charity by naming it "Captain Alving's Home." In an ironic reflection on the immorality of both himself and the unfaithful Captain Alving, he describes the home as the sort of place where "a man might feel under a father's eye."

Regina Engstrand

During the course of this play, Regina's character changes from that of the doting servant who is in love with the master of the house to that of a cold manipulator. She is the first character on the stage. When Engstrand comes in, she shows concern for Oswald, who is napping upstairs. Engstrand wants to include Regina in his scheme to open a tavern, offering her money to be made and the opportunity to marry a rich man, or to be paid off by a rich man who gets her pregnant, and Regina is offended by the offer. When Mrs. Alving invites Regina to sit down and have some champagne with her and Oswald at the end of Act II, Regina thinks she is being treated as one of the family because she is to marry Oswald, unaware that she is part of the family because she is Oswald's sister.

In the last act, when she is told that she is the daughter of Captain Alving, Regina immediately asks to leave. Her concern for Oswald turns out to have been built on what he could do for her, and so she has decided immediately that there is nothing to help her ambitions.

Pastor Manders

Throughout the play, the pastor speaks for conventional morality, even though he does not seem to deeply believe in the course of action that convention would require. This is made most clear in his deliberation over whether or not to insure the orphanage. He says that he would not have any problem with insuring it, but that it might cause a scandal among people who might see insurance as a sign that he does not have enough faith in God to keep the building safe. He is so afraid of the prospect of scandal that he advises against insurance.

Reality is not of primary concern to Pastor Manders. In Act II, when Mrs. Alving has regrets about not having told Oswald how disreputable his father was, Manders takes the position that it was more important to give the boy ideals than to tell him the truth. This concern for inner serenity over understanding what actually happened may account for why he so adamantly denies the attraction that

Mrs. Alving says once was mutual.

Because he is more concerned with appearance than with true moral behavior, Pastor Manders is a dupe for Engstrand, who address the pastor humbly as "your Reverence" and pretends to defer to Manders, all the while having his way. As a result of not being able to see when Engstrand is being false, Manders actually believes that he has struggled against being a lazy drunkard, although he has no evidence of this except Engstrand's word. In the end, he believes Engstrand's claim that he saw Manders start the fire with the candle, even though the pastor does not remember holding a candle in his hand, and he runs away from all of his responsibilities in the town, rather than face up to the possible negative opinion that would follow from the fire.

reputation

pillar of society

pastor mander too assimilate into the action... by highority

MORALITY IS ON A CORRUPT BASIS

Themes

Deception

The main conflict of this play stems from the fact that Mrs. Alving feels remorse for her part in helping to deceive the world about what sort of man Captain Alving was. She feels that she should have told the truth to Oswald long ago. If she had been honest with him all along, the disease that he inherited from his father may still have been unavoidable, but she could have saved him the confusion that he felt upon finding out that his father, who he thought was morally pure, had syphilis. His own character might have been less cynical if the truth about his father had not come as such a shock.

For his part, Pastor Manders supports the idea of deception. When Mrs. Alving talks about truth, he counters her with talk about ideals. He tells her that, regardless of what the true facts are, Oswald needs to have ideals, that she should not sour his image of his father if that is something that Oswald thinks he can believe in.

Media Adaptations

- *Ghosts* was adapted as a silent film in 1915, starring Erich von Stroheim and Mary Alden. It was produced by D. W. Griffith.

- There is a modern version, produced in 1986, with Judi Dench as Mrs. Alving, Kenneth Branagh as Oswald, and Natasha Richardson as Regina. Elijah Moshinsky directed.

- An unabridged audio cassette, with Flo Gibson reading it as text (not "performing" it as a play) was released in 1993 by Audio Book Contractors of Washington, D. C.

In the end, the pastor's belief in deception turns against him. Because his own ideal is that

Engstrand is basically a decent, if weak, person, he is more willing to believe what Engstrand says about the fire at the orphanage than what he himself remembers. Pastor Manders falls for a simple deception almost willingly because his grasp on truth is so completely flexible.

Loyalty

In *Ghosts,* the only true loyalty is between Mrs. Alving and her son. All other instances of loyalty seem pure, but they are actually based in social usefulness. The first example of this sort of insincere loyalty is in the early scene between Engstrand and Regina. He asks her to help him with the sailors' home, making a feigned attempt to be concerned about her because she is his daughter. He is not intelligent enough, however, to stick with his case and eventually admits that he wants her there because it would be good for business to have a woman around. Later, he is just as transparently insincere about his loyalty when he tells Manders, "Jacob Engstrand may be likened to a guardian angel, he may, your Reverence." The danger that he professes to "guard" the parson against is the charge that he burned down the orphanage, which is a charge that Engstrand himself made up.

Topics for Further Study

- Parallels have been drawn between this play's treatment of syphilis and the current AIDS epidemic. Make a list of suggestions of changes that would have to be made to *Ghosts* if it were to be played as if Oswald had AIDS.

- Write a short scene taking place between Captain Alving and Mrs. Alving, giving your audience a sense of the tension in their household when she was trying to control his cheating.

- When Pastor Manders says that Johanna was a fallen woman when she was married, Mrs. Alving points out that, using the same reasoning, Captain Alving was a fallen man. In small groups, discuss how much people make such sexists distinctions in contemporary America.

- The last scene of *Ghosts* deals with mercy killing, a subject that has become even more pertinent as medicine has learned to extend the lives of terminally ill people. Research outside sources that have weighed in on the euthanasia debate and write a paper explaining what you think Mrs. Alving should do about Oswald.

- Research the world of Parisian artists in the 1870s and 1880s. Was their worldwide reputation for loose morals deserved? Give some examples that Ibsen might have had in mind when he was writing this play.

Manders claims to be loyal to the sanctity of marriage. When discussing the time when Helena Alving came to his home after leaving his husband, though, his main focus is on the possible scandal that could have ensued. He's less motivated by loyalty to religious and social doctrine than by fear of repercussions.

Oswald pretends to be loyal to Regina, the maid, but later on, after he reveals the facts about his disease, he talks about how he has counted on her to look after him when his disease makes him an invalid. Regina, for her part, professes her loyalty to Oswald until she finds out that they cannot be married and that he is ill. These are good reasons to not marry him and to realize that they will not have the relationship that she thought they would have, but she is extreme in tossing her loyalty aside, making plans to leave the house the very minute that she hears the news.

Moral Corruption

Ibsen uses Oswald's disease to symbolize the corruption that is handed down from previous generations. When he tells his mother about being diagnosed, Oswald even quotes the doctor as making a statement that indicates a moral judgment beyond his medical one: "The sins of the fathers are visited on the children." This makes sense because, in a strictly physical sense, it is Captain Alving's blood that infected his unborn son. It makes just as much sense in a completely moral frame, too, because Oswald, after finding out that his father was sexually active, took on many of the same qualities. The facts that he smokes his father's pipe, that he drinks constantly, and especially that he flirts with the family maid, just as his father did, are all directly related to being his father's son. Ibsen uses the transmission of the syphilis infection to represent the fact that immorality passes from generation to generation as if it were a genetic condition.

The way that morality is carried through a family is also examined in the example of Regina. Throughout much of the play, she behaves as her mother did: she is a maid, conspicuously at the same house where her mother worked, and she is willing to be the mistress of a wealthy man to get what she wants. When she finds out that she is Captain Alving's daughter, she refers to the Sailor's Home that is named after him as "one house where I've every right to a place." It is not a decent place for a woman, but her connection with Engstrand and with the Captain make it her birthright.

Pastor Manders worries that Mrs. Alving will be morally corrupted by reading new, free-thinking ideas, but the readings that he finds dangerous make her feel more secure. Rather than corrupting her, they just let her know that she is not alone in the way she sees things: as she tells him, "I seem to find explanation and confirmation of all sorts of things that I myself have been thinking."

Victim and Victimization

Ibsen's style of realism does not allow for even the most downtrodden of characters to look like a victim. The most tragic figure in the play is Oswald, who suffers from a disease that was contracted by his father and who did not know that he was infected, did not even think that he could be infected, for much of his life. Still, his condition cannot be called victimization because his is not a decent personality that is being taken advantage of.

At heart, Oswald is self-centered. He hates the thought of being ill because it will incapacitate him, and he is full of life. His attitude toward his mother is best summarized when he says, "you can be so very useful to me, now that I'm ill." His relationship with Regina, too, is based on what she can do to help him in his illness. In a sense, the victim of the inherited venereal disease uses his misfortune to justify victimizing everyone around him.

In the course of the play, Mrs. Alving comes to reconsider her relationship with Captain Alving. At first, she tells Pastor Manders of the ways in which she was the captain's victim. She describes her life with and without him, as a life and death struggle to keep Oswald from knowing his father's true nature, although she later calls herself a coward for not telling him the truth. She describes the measures that she took to keep him home nights, so that he would not ruin his reputation by going to town and chasing women. She later regrets her actions, taking the responsibility on herself instead of blaming him for her actions; in fact, by the final act she sees him as her victim, because she suppressed "the overpowering joy of life that was in him."

Realism

Realism, as a literary movement, flourished in the United States and Europe in the late 1800s, which is when *Ghosts* was written. In response to romanticism, which presented a version of reality that was twisted through human perception, realism marked an attempt to capture the truth about life, especially the ugly elements of truth that people would rather ignore. Realist literature is often associated with suffering, with disease and corruption, because these are the elements of life that romantic literature shied away from. *Ghosts* comes from a period in Ibsen's career that is considered his realist period, during which he wrote about social issues that disturbed him and his audience, with the hope that examining such unpleasant truths would lead to social change. In this play, he is unmasking the hypocrisy that is usually behind memorials to great civic leaders, looking at the damage that a man with a great reputation might leave in his wake, the "ghosts" that linger.

Setting

All three acts of this play take place in the same setting: the garden-room of Mrs. Alving's house. Keeping the action contained to this one place gives the play several distinguishing aspects. First, the small, enclosed, limited set keeps audiences' attention focused on the characters and how they are interacting with one another. The human drama takes precedence over the exterior trappings that are necessary, but incidental.

This one particular location is meaningful because it is where the past, which affects the present in a ghostly way, took place. This house is where Captain Alving lived; through the doors is the dining room where Helena Alving saw him accost the maid; the bleak fjords on the landscape outside of the windows have defined Mrs. Alving's world for most of her life. No other set would convey as much about what life was like in that house thirty years earlier, when the Alvings were newlyweds, when the trouble all began. If ghosts haunt this family, this specific setting is the locus of their haunting ground.

Symbolism

A writer of Ibsen's caliber will always present objects that resonate with meaning beyond their actual function in the play. In *Ghosts,* several stand out as particularly noteworthy. The most obvious is the orphanage. An orphanage is, of course, a place for children who are left alone in the world without parents. By erecting an orphanage as a memorial, Mrs. Alving is able to accomplish two aims at once. She creates a public institution that benefits the community and enhances the prestige of the person it is named after, but, in making the memorial an orphanage, she also creates a subtle, sarcastic commentary on how the captain treated his own children. In the course of the play, the orphanage, which was to be a tribute to a man who did not deserve one, burns down, indicating that such deception is destined to fail.

The second most important symbolic element is Oswald's disease. Although the script does not name it, the symptoms match those of syphilis. Two aspects of syphilis make it symbolically important in a story like this. The first is the fact that it is spread through intercourse; Captain Alving would never have had the disease if he had been the morally proper man that he and those around him pretended he was. The second aspect is that it can be passed down from parents to unborn children'as Oswald quotes his doctor, "The sins of the father are visited upon the children." There is also a biblical reference to the doctrine of Original Sin, which states that all humans are born sinful because of the sin of the first human, Adam. The doctor, after examining him, told Oswald, "You have been worm-eated from your birth."

A minor, but significant, object that has meaning beyond its actual existence is the champagne glass. In Act II, Regina is invited to drink champagne with Mrs. Alving and Oswald. Because she is the maid, she is apprehensive, but since she does have hopes of marrying Oswald she can believe that the invitation is legitimate. Before they can drink, though, they are interrupted, first by the entrance of Pastor Manders and then by the orphanage burning in the distance. When they come back from the fire, the champagne bottle is still unopened, and Mrs. Alving tells Oswald and Regina that he is her brother. Before leaving the house, Regina takes a bitter glance at the champagne that she was not able to have and remarks, "I may come to drink champagne with gentlefolks yet." Although she lived there and, as she tells Engstrand in the first act, was "treated almost as a daughter here," drinking champagne represents a class barrier that she has been unable to cross.

Norway in the 1880s

Ibsen lived away from Norway from 1863 to 1891. Rather than distancing him from the character of the Norwegian people, though, critics note that this separation helped him understand his native land better. Throughout the 1800s, Norway was a land of peaceful self-assurance, left alone to rule itself while still formally under the control of Sweden. This period of independence was a result of the Napoleonic Wars, which changed the organization of Scandinavia as much as they changed almost all of Europe's political structure. Norway had been a province of Denmark for several centuries, from 1381 to 1814, but was taken from Norway, which supported Napoleon, and given over to Swedish rule because Sweden had supported the Russians, who eventually defeated the French. Sweden allowed Norway a great deal of independence. The Norwegian constitution, drafted in 1815, gave more political power to the Norwegian king's council than to ministers from Sweden, whose power was limited to advising. Norway came to be one of Europe's most independent and also one of its wealthiest countries, with the third largest merchant navy on the planet.

One result of this peace, prosperity, and independence was that social issues were examined with greater seriousness than they were in countries just struggling for subsistence. Issues of moral conduct were examined by radical social organizations that would have been outlawed in stricter countries. Also, questions of marriage and sexuality, which would have been left to church decree in the Catholic countries of Europe, were open to discussion in Norway, which was predominantly Lutheran. *Ghosts* was still a shock to Norwegian audiences when it debuted, but it would have been unthinkable to raise some of the issues it raises in a less progressive country.

Realism

Ibsen is considered one of the most important figures in the realist movement that came to dominate literature in Europe and America in the last half of the 1800s. Realism was a reaction to romanticism, which dominated the first half of the century. The romantic movement was about individual freedom—the most important writers of that period generally shared the belief that reality was flexible, subject to human interpretation. Beauty was assumed to have its own distinct existence, aside from the world people live in, and it was assumed that people had the power to interpret reality as they saw fit. Leading romantic writers were the poets Keats and Shelly, the essayist Henry Wadsworth Longfellow, and Edgar Allan Poe. After a while, romantic idealism came to be seen as too dependent on wishful thinking and not connected strongly enough to reality. The realist movement took romantic principles and, in effect, reversed them.

Realism recognized that individuals do not control their environment, but most struggle with it constantly. Realist ideas are evident in *Ghosts* in the way that the reality of disease puts a stop to Oswald's artistic ambitions, and the ways that social expectations put limits on what Mrs. Alving is able to do with her life. It was a time when the invisible rules of social interaction were being explored. Charles Darwin's theory of evolution defined the capabilities of the body and drew attention to heredity; Karl Marx proposed the principles of historic inevitability; Sigmund Freud worked at mapping the unseen mechanism of the mind. In the arts, realists like Ibsen, Tolstoy, and Zola did not shy away from showing the miseries that followed when the free-thinking individual was hemmed in by society, but they usually showed misery for a purpose, to shake up old expectations and move people to demand change.

Compare & Contrast

- **1882:** German engineer Gottlieb Daimler invents the first internal combustion engine.

  Today: Automobiles are so common that they create constant problems of crowding and pollution in urban and suburban areas around the globe.

- **1882:** Major industrial areas, such as New York and London, are experimenting with electrical lighting to replace gas lights.

  Today: Most areas in the world have been reached with electrical cables from huge nuclear or hydroelectric generators.

- **1882:** The first birth control clinic in the world is opened in Amsterdam by Aletta Jacobs, who is the first woman to practice medicine in Holland.

  Today: Birth control is still a controversial subject, even in areas where the rates of birth to single mothers have skyrocketed.

- **1882:** Six years after Alexander Graham Bell develops the first working telephone, Western Electric began producing telephone units.

  Today: Wireless telephones and e-mail devices that use the same radio waves are among the most popular consumer products.

- **1882:** The romantic image of the western outlaw is developed after the death of Jesse James, a bank robber who was killed by his cousin for reward money.

Today: Criminal figures are still romanticized in popular culture, particularly in rap music.

- **1882:** Chicago, where *Ghosts* premiered, installs its first mechanized form of public transportation: electric cable cars that can travel twenty blocks along a straight street in half an hour.

Today: Underground trains and elevated trains can take passengers out of the city to the airport in that same amount of time.

Syphilis

Syphilis is an infectious disease, seldom fatal today but incurable in Ibsen's time. It is usually spread by sexual intercourse with an infected person; because the spirochete that carries the disease cannot live very long in the open, it is almost impossible for syphilis to be transmitted without an exchange of bodily fluids. The first known cases of syphilis in Europe occurred in 1493, leading medical historians to believe that the disease was brought back to the continent by the crew of Christopher Columbus' first expedition to the Americas in 1492. In the following decades, it became a major disease. Its symptoms are similar to those of other diseases, which led to constant confusion about its characteristics before a blood test for diagnosing the disease was developed in 1905. Ibsen's use of the disease in *Ghosts* shows several misconceptions about syphilis, most notably the idea that a child born with it can develop symptoms as late as his twenties; infected newborns sometimes do not develop symptoms until a few weeks after birth, but it does not lie dormant for years.

The first effective treatment for syphilis was developed in 1909, when German-born bacteriologist Paul Ehrlich found that the compound Salvarsan was effective in killing off the spirochete that caused it. Unfortunately, Salvarsan contained arsenic, a deadly poison. In 1943, penicillin was found highly effective as a treatment, and that method is used today. Using an antibiotic program centered on penicillin, doctors have the power to contain syphilis, but in treating the disease scientists are confronted with public attitudes. People with the disease sometimes put off treatment, afraid or ashamed because of its connection with sexual promiscuity. As a result, not all treatable cases are reported to doctors early enough to be cured.

Critical Overview

At the time when he wrote *Ghosts,* Ibsen's career had eased into a phase of social criticism. His previous work, *A Doll's House,* was met with some objection, but it is easily his most popular and influential play to date. Today, critics consider Ibsen one of the most important playwrights of the modern period, pivotal in introducing a new, realistic way of presenting life on the stage. With the publication of *Ghosts,* though, his career almost came to a grinding halt.

Of all of Ibsen's dramas, *Ghosts* is easily the most controversial, crammed tight with social and sexual themes that challenged the conventional morality. Readers rejected the play and refused to buy it when it was released in book form. Theatrical companies also found it too dangerous to risk offending their local communities. Most of the copies printed in the first edition were returned to the publisher, and they did not all sell for thirteen years. As Ibsen biographer Hans Heiberg explains in a chapter titled, "The Great Scandal":

> From December 1881 and throughout the whole of 1882, a hurricane continued to blow all through Scandinavia over Ibsen's new play. And it was not only the conservatives who let out a howl. The liberals, too, and most radicals,

were so shaken by the explosion that they neither realized what a masterpiece it was, nor that there was balance in it. Most people thought that Ibsen, through the mouth of Mrs. Alving, wanted to legalize incest and advocate sexual license and nihilism.

Scandanavian theaters would not put the play on, and its debut occurred across the ocean, in Chicago, which had a large Norwegian population. Eventually, a company directed by August Lindberg had success with the play in Helsinki, and their subsequent tour met with increasing popularity.

In the following decade, Ibsen's reputation as a masterful playwright who challenged conventions had become even more solidified by his successes with *An Enemy of the People*(1882) and *Hedda Gabler*(1890). William Archer, Ibsen's contemporary, recognized *Ghosts'* power in capturing reality, and dismissed its critics for trying to limit what an artist can write about. "If art is ever debarred from entering upon certain domains of human experience," he wrote in 1889,"then *Ghosts* is an inartistic work. I can only say, after having read it, seen it on the stage, and translated it, that no other modern play seems to me to fulfill so entirely the Aristotelian ideal of purging the soul by means of terror and pity." The unpleasant elements, in other words, were good for audiences, who could free themselves of their own problems through the act of watching.

Because of his strongly-stated political views,

Ibsen became a favorite of political activists, who advocated change in almost all areas of life, from woman's rights to socialism to sexual freedom. Early in the twentieth century, Ibsen's works, especially *Ghosts,* were hailed as heroic achievements, as political unrest against the status quo swelled in Europe and in America. A prime example is Emma Goldman, possibly America's most famous anarchist, who devoted considerable space to the play in her 1914 book *The Social Significance of Modern Drama.*"The social and revolutionary significance of Henrik Ibsen is brought out with even greater force in *Ghosts* than in his preceding works," Goldman wrote. "Not only does this pioneer of modern dramatic art undermine in *Ghosts* the Social Lie and the paralyzing effect of Duty, but the uselessness and evil of Sacrifice, the dreary Lack of Joy and of Purpose in Work are brought to light as most pernicious and destructive elements of life." The end of her review was filled with just as much praise, bordering on hyperbole:

> The voice of Henrik Ibsen in [this play] sounds like the trumpets before the walls of Jericho. Into the remotest nooks and corners reaches his voice, with its thundering indictment of our moral cancers, our social poisons, our hideous crimes against unborn and born victims. Verily a more revolutionary condemnation has never been uttered in dramatic form before or since the great Henrik Ibsen.

Martin Esslin, one of the most respected and influential contemporary writers about drama, notes in his book about Ibsen that the great German playwright Bertolt Brecht considered *Ghosts* to have been rendered obsolete by 1928, owing to medical developments in suppressing syphilis. The play has continued, however, because audiences do not look at it as an old-fashioned criticism of our time, as Brecht might have, but as a work that was surprisingly ahead of its own time, that has kept its edge by emphasizing human attitudes over situations. Esslin emphasizes how Ibsen changed the performing world by having characters express their motivation gradually and indirectly through dialogue and action. This is something that audiences take for granted today, but the style of Ibsen's contemporaries called for characters whose motivations were obvious the moment that they stepped out on stage. Esslin traces the development of this technique of spontaneity from Ibsen through Chekhov and the Moscow Theatre to modern avant-garde filmmakers like John Cassavettes and Robert Altaian, as well as playwrights like Eugene Ionesco and Harold Pinter, whose characters rely on more than just their words to convey who they are.

What Do I Read Next?

- Ibsen's play *An Enemy of the People* was started before *Ghosts* but was not finished until after the latter play. It is a scathing indictment of social standards, as a doctor who points out contamination of a town's water supply goes from hero to enemy when his revelation upsets the local economy. Viking Press has a 1987 edition edited by Arthur Miller, the author of *Death of a Salesman*.

- At the same time that Ibsen wrote in Norway, August Strindberg was the leading playwright in Sweden. Both playwrights explored the new realistic forms. *Miss Julie,* Strindberg's 1888 drama about an aristocratic girl and her affair with her conniving butler, is considered his best.

- The Russian author Anton Chekhov is considered one of the greatest authors of short stories and dramas in history. He cited Ibsen as one of his main influences. All of Chekhov's plays are important, but *The Cherry Orchard*(1904) in particular examines some of the same themes as *Ghosts*.

- Irish playwright George Bernard Shaw was a supporter of moderate Socialist ideas. His political analysis of Ibsen is printed as a book, *The Quintessence of Ibsenism,* available in a 1994 Dover Books edition.

- Ibsen's life and ideas come alive in the 1970 publication *Correspondence of Henrik Ibsen,* edited by Mary Morrison.

- The way that writers treat the weaknesses of the body, like Ibsen's use of syphilis to represent the decadence that is passed down from one generation to the next, was examined in Susan Sontag's classic essay *Illness as a Metaphor,* which is now published in one volume (1995) with its sequel, *AIDS and Its Metaphors*.

- Stella Adler is one of the great teachers of actors in America, having been instrumental in the training of Marlon Brando, Robert DeNiro, Al Pacino, and others. In 1999, Barry Paris edited a series of her lectures into one cohesive book, *Stella Adler on Ibsen, Strindberg and Chekhov.*

Sources

Archer, William, "Ibsen and English Criticism," in *Fortnightly Review,* Vol. 46, No. 271, July, 1889, pp. 30-37.

Derry, T. K., *A History of Scandinavia,* University of Minnesota Press, 1979.

Esslin, Martin, "Ibsen and Modern Drama," in *Ibsen and the Theater: The Dramatist in Production,* New York University Press, 1980, pp. 71-82.

Goldman, Emma, *The Social Significance of Modern Drama,* Gorham Press, 1914.

Heiberg, Hans, in *Ibsen: A Portrait of the Artist,* translated by Joan Tate, University of Miami Press, 1987, p. 217.

Further Reading

Archer, William, ed., *From Ibsen's Workshop: Notes, Scenarios and Drafts of the Modern Plays,* translated by A. G. Charter, Scribner, 1978.

> This reprint of the 1913 study shows the process of development of Ibsen's most important works. Included is an introduction by Archer, who was one of Ibsen's most knowledgeable critics.

Clurman, Harold, "In Full Stride," in *Ibsen,* Macmillan Publishing Co., 1977.

> A chapter in Clurman's critical survey of Ibsen, which covers *Ghosts* and *A Doll's House.* This analysis examines the approach actors need to take in order to fully understand the characters in the play.

Joyce, James, "Ibsen's New Drama," from *The Critical Writings of James Joyce,* Viking Penguin, 1959.

> Originally published in 1900, this review of a minor, seldom-discussed Ibsen piece, *When We Dead Awaken,* touches on all of the plays in the author's long career.

Lebowitz, Naomi, *Ibsen and the Great World,* Louisiana State University Press, 1990.

> This book is an in-depth look at how Ibsen's environment shaped his characterizations. Difficult and rich.

MacFarlane, James, ed., *The Cambridge Companion to Ibsen,* Cambridge University Press, 1994.

> An indispensable guide, with cross-references to all of Ibsen's major works and annotations about the references made in them. MacFarlane, who oversaw the publication, is one of the world's great authorities on Ibsen.

Meyer, Hans Georg, "Ibsen's Dramatic Technique," in *Henrik Ibsen,* Frederick Ungar Publishing Co., 1972, pp. 9-18.

> Focuses mostly on the earlier plays *Brand* and *Peer Gynt* to draw generalizations about how Ibsen's style evolved throughout the different phases of his life.

Salome, Lou, *Ibsen's Heroines,* Black Swan Books, 1985.

> For thorough appreciation, the chapter about the main character of *Ghosts* should be read along with Salome's analyses of Ibsen's other important female characters.

Theoharis, Constantine, *Ibsen's Drama: Right Action and Tragic Joy,* St. Martin's Press, 1996.

Theoharis delves deeply into the underlying psychology of each of the characters and how their interlocking needs hold the plays together.

CPSIA information can be obtained
at www.ICGtesting.com
Printed in the USA
BVHW041709040321
601750BV00008B/29

9 781375 380492